Y0-BWE-772

Christmas Songs of Joy

EASY PIANO
Arranged by DAN COATES

Cover Photo: © Index Stock Photography Inc.
Project Manager: Carol Cuellar

Dan Coates

One of today's foremost personalities in the field of printed music, Dan Coates has been providing teachers and professional musicians with quality piano material since 1975. Equally adept in arranging for beginners or accomplished musicians, his Big Note, Easy Piano and Professional Touch arrangements have made a significant contribution to the industry.

Born in Syracuse, New York, Dan began to play piano at age four. By the time he was 15, he'd won a New York State competition for music composers. After high school graduation, he toured the United States, Canada and Europe as an arranger and pianist with the world-famous group "Up With People".

Dan settled in Miami, Florida, where he studied piano with Ivan Davis at the University of Miami while playing professionally throughout southern Florida. To date, his performance credits include appearances on "Murphy Brown," "My Sister Sam" and at the Opening Ceremonies of the 1984 Summer Olympics in Los Angeles. Dan has also accompanied such artists as Dusty Springfield and Charlotte Rae.

In 1982, Dan began his association with Warner Bros. Publications - an association which has produced more than 400 Dan Coates books and sheets. Throughout the year he conducts piano workshops nation-wide, during which he demonstrates his popular arrangements.

Contents

HAVE YOURSELF
A MERRY LITTLE CHRISTMAS

Words and Music by
HUGH MARTIN and
RALPH BLANE
Arranged by DAN COATES

LET IT SNOW! LET IT SNOW! LET IT SNOW!

Lyric by
SAMMY CAHN

Music by
JULE STYNE
Arranged by DAN COATES

DECK THE HALL

Traditional Old Welsh
Arranged by DAN COATES

Joyfully

Deck the halls with boughs of hol - ly.

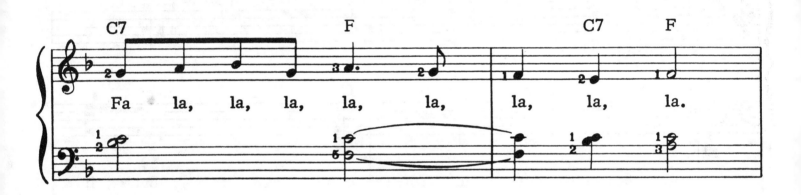

Fa la, la, la, la, la, la, la, la.

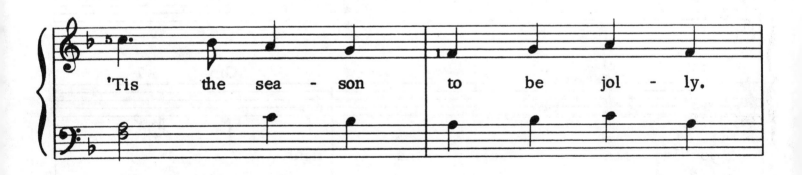

'Tis the sea - son to be jol - ly.

Fa la, la, la, la, la, la, la, la.

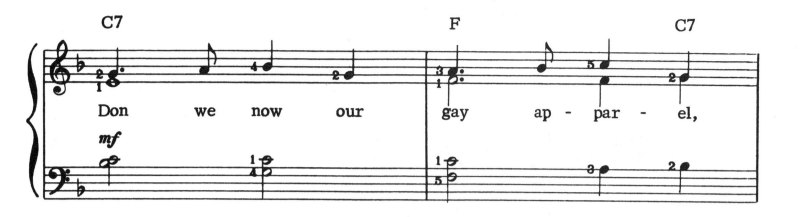

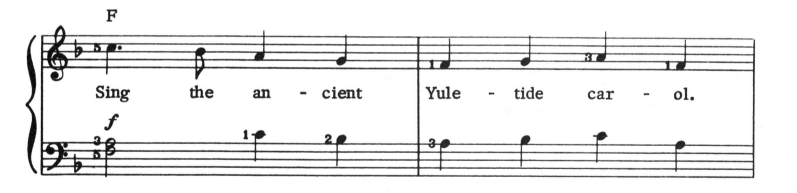

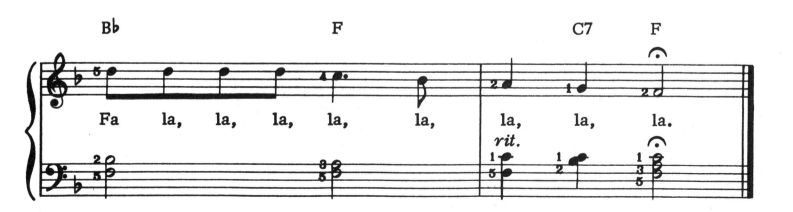

JOY TO THE WORLD

Words by
ISAAC WATTS

Music by
GEORGE F. HANDEL
Arranged by DAN COATES

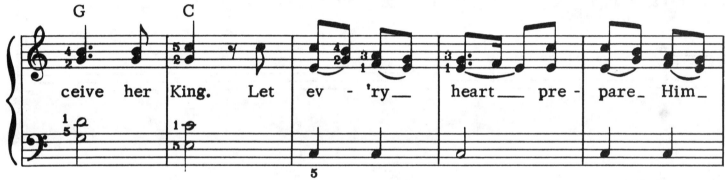

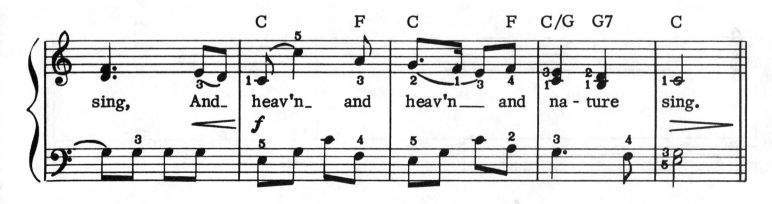

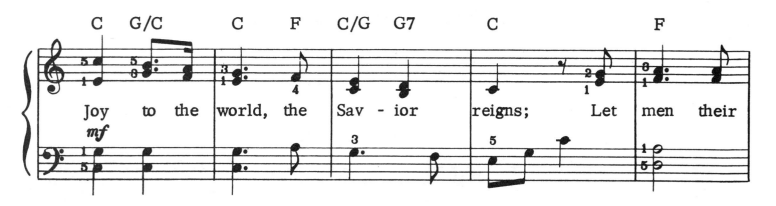

Joy to the world, the Sav - ior reigns; Let men their

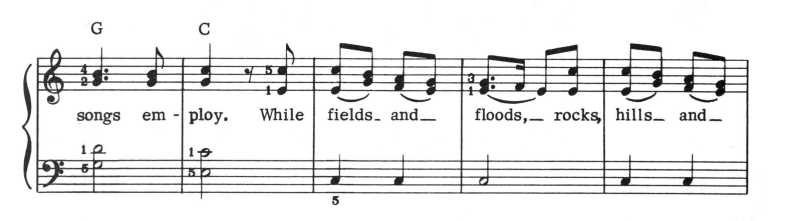

songs em - ploy. While fields_ and_ floods,_ rocks, hills_ and_

plains,_ Re - peat the sound-ing_ joy, Re - peat the sound-ing_

joy, Re - peat_ re - peat _ the sound-ing joy!

JINGLE BELLS

Traditional
Arranged by DAN COATES

15

RUDOLPH,
THE RED-NOSED REINDEER

Words and Music by
JOHNNY MARKS
Arranged by DAN COATES

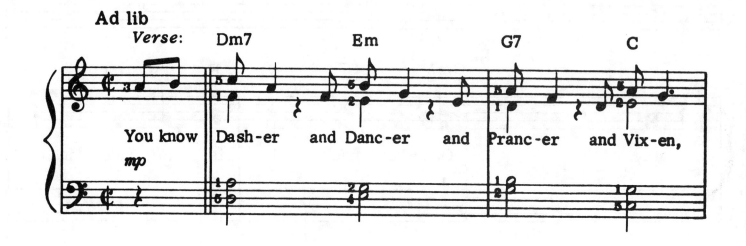

Lightly

Chorus:

Ru-dolph, the red-nosed | rein - deer | had a ver - y shin - y
All of the oth - er | rein - deer | used to laugh and call him

nose. | And if you ev - er | saw it,
names, | they nev - er let poor | Ru - dolph

1. you would ev-en say it glows.

2. join in an - y rein - deer

games. | Then one fog - gy | Christ-mas Eve, | San - ta came to

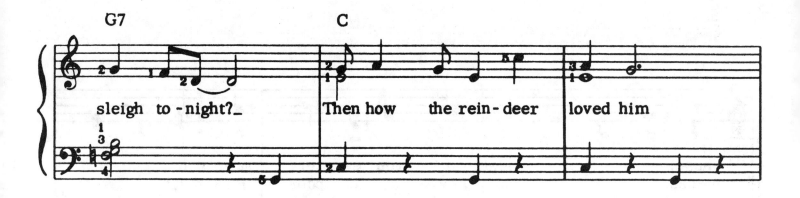

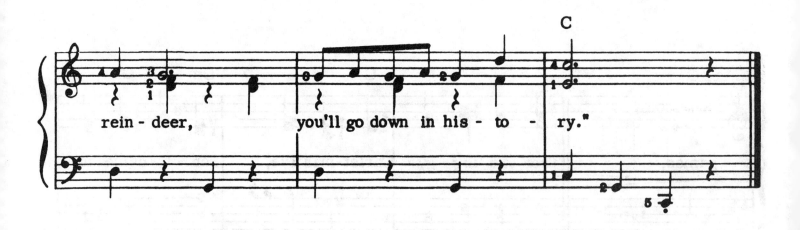

WINTER WONDERLAND

Words by
DICK SMITH

Music by
FELIX BERNARD
Arranged by DAN COATES

Moderately ... Sleigh bells ring, are you lis - t'nin'? In the lane, snow is

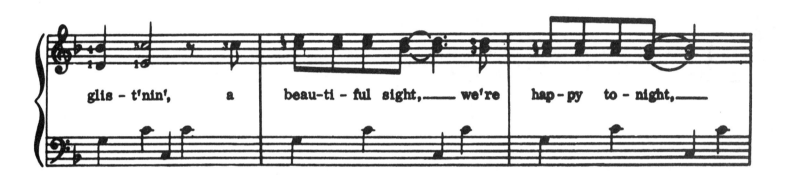

glis - t'nin', a beau-ti - ful sight,___ we're hap-py to - night,___

walk - in' in a win-ter won-der- land! Gone a - way is the

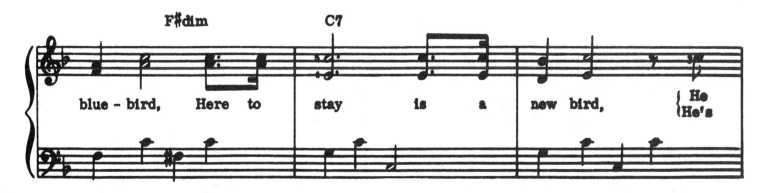

blue - bird, Here to stay is a new bird, He / He's

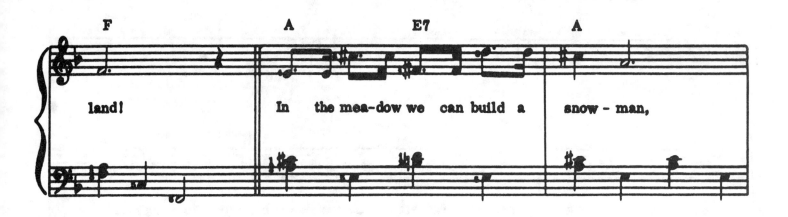

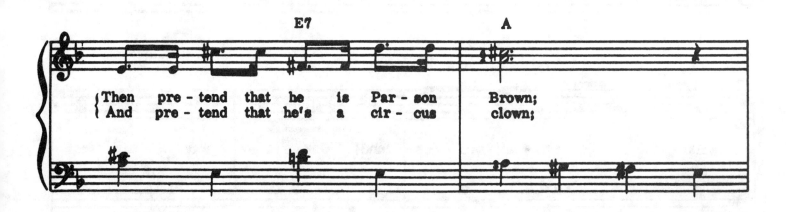

ALL I WANT FOR CHRISTMAS IS
MY TWO FRONT TEETH

Words and Music by
DON GARDNER
Arranged by DAN COATES

ANGELS FROM THE REALMS OF GLORY

Words by
JAMES MONTGOMERY

Music by
HENRY SMART
Arranged by DAN COATES

1. An - gels from the realms of glo - ry,
2. Shep - herds in the field a - bid - ing,
3. Sag - es, leave your con - tem - pla - tions,

Wing your flight o'er all the earth.
Watch - ing o'er your flocks by night,
Bright - er vi - sions beam a - far;

Ye, who sang cre - a - tion's sto - ry,
God with man is now re - sid - ing,
Seek the great De - sire of na - tions,

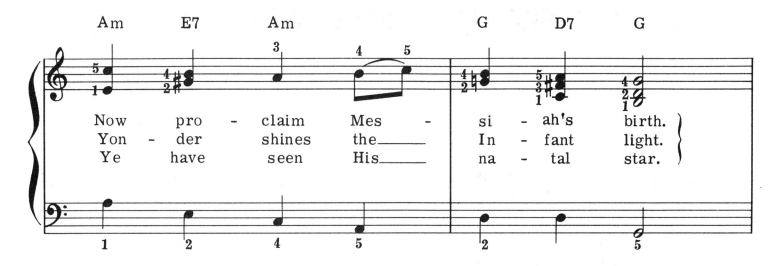

Now pro - claim Mes - si - ah's birth.
Yon - der shines the___ In - fant light.
Ye have seen His___ na - tal star.

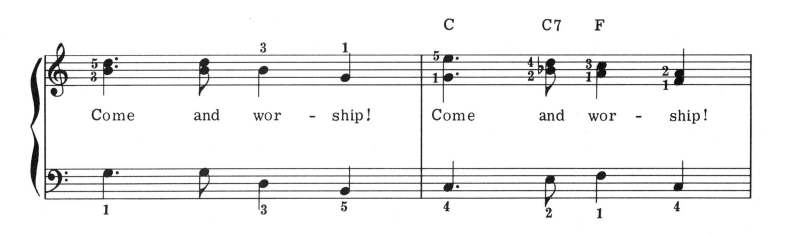

Come and wor - ship! Come and wor - ship!

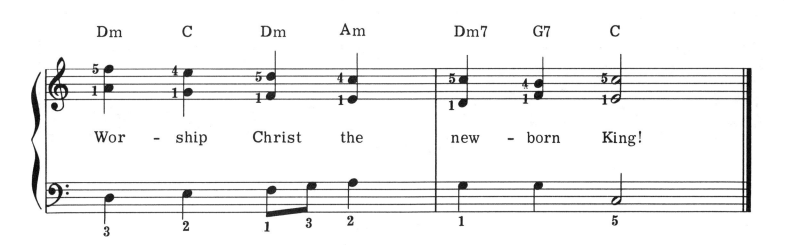

Wor - ship Christ the new - born King!

ANGELS WE HAVE HEARD ON HIGH

Traditional
Arranged by DAN COATES

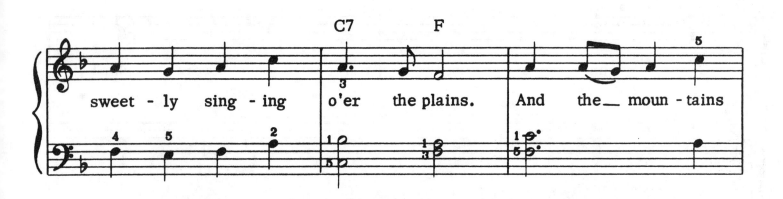

AWAY IN A MANGER

By
MARTIN LUTHER
Arranged by DAN COATES

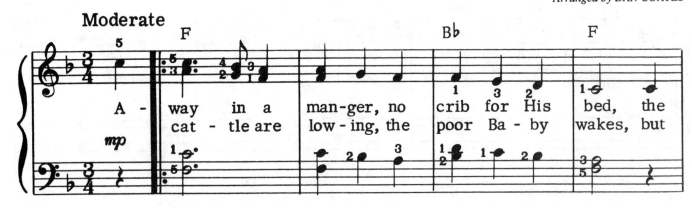

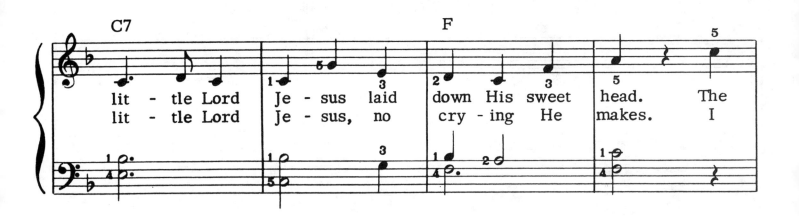

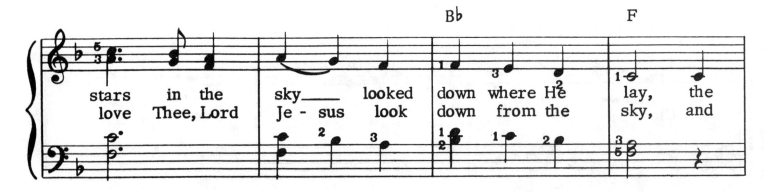

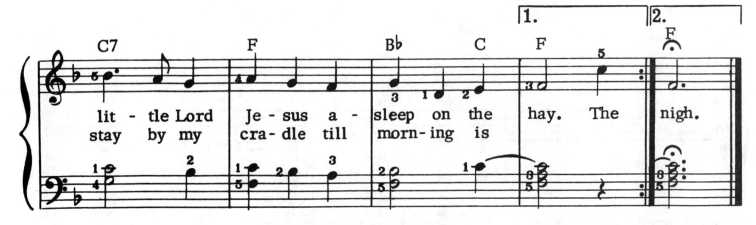

THE COVENTRY CAROL

Traditional Catalonian Carol
Arranged by DAN COATES

THE BIRTHDAY OF A KING

By
WILLIAM H. NEIDLINGER
Arranged by DAN COATES

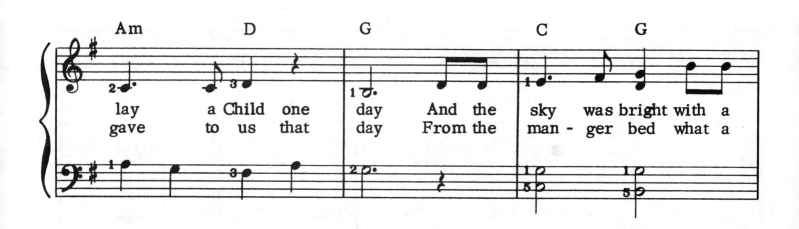

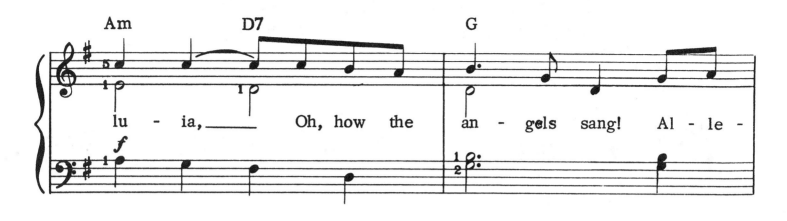

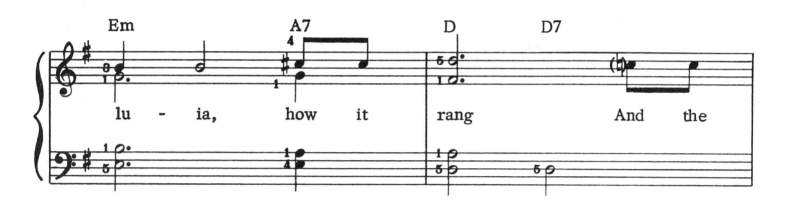

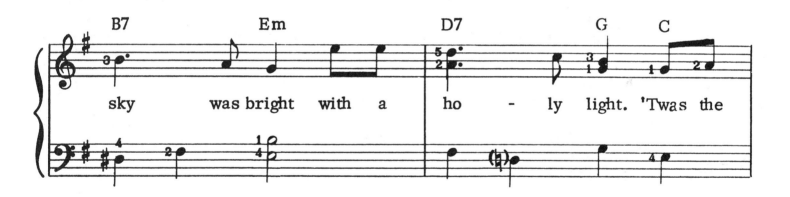

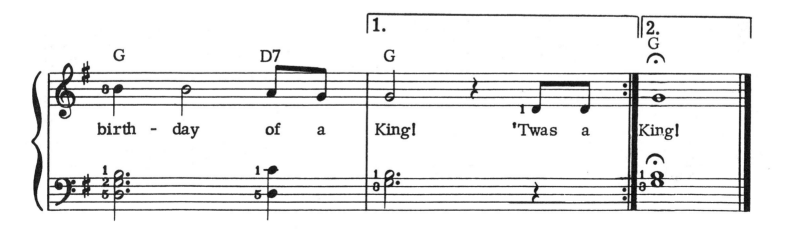

THE BOAR'S HEAD CAROL

Ancient Oxford Carol
XVI Century
Arranged by DAN COATES

GLAD CHRISTMAS BELLS

Traditional
Arranged by DAN COATES

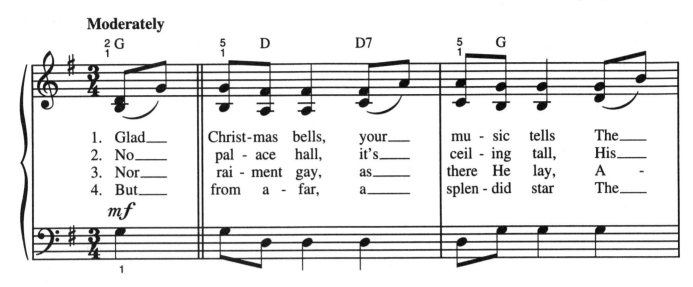

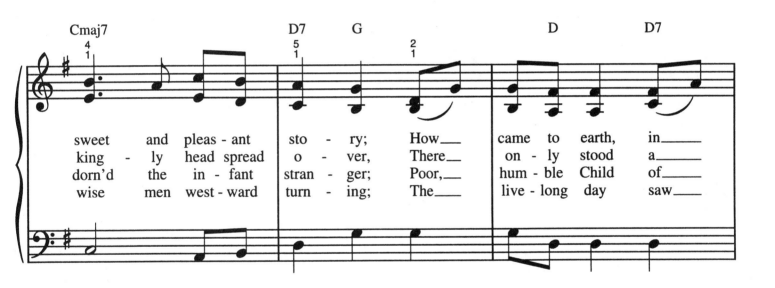

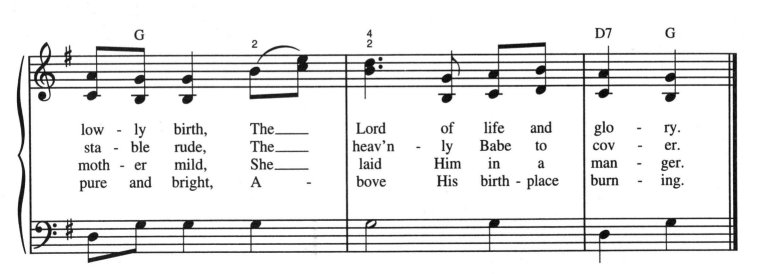

A CHILD THIS DAY IS BORN

Traditonal
English
Arranged by DAN COATES

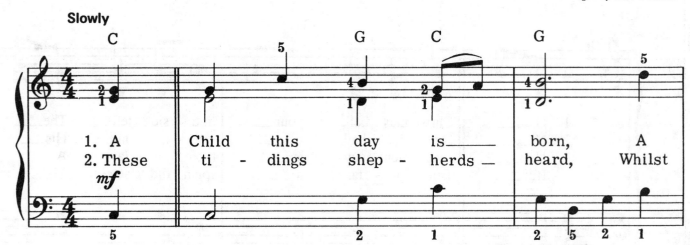

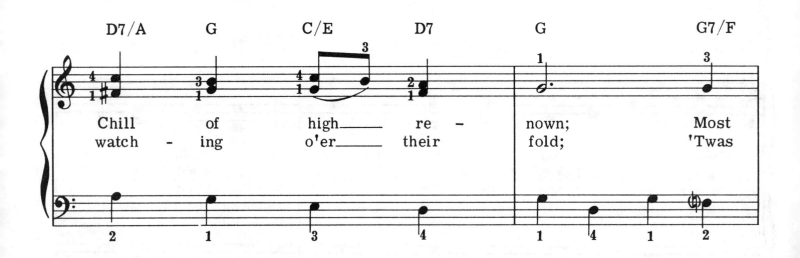

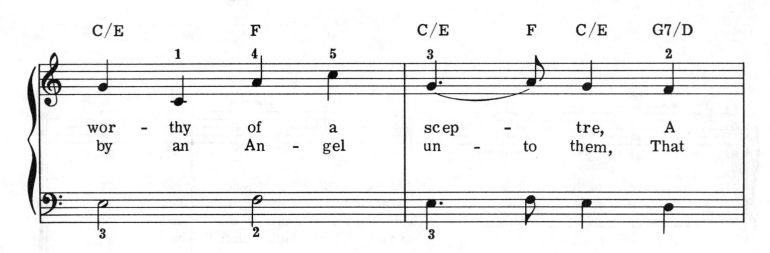

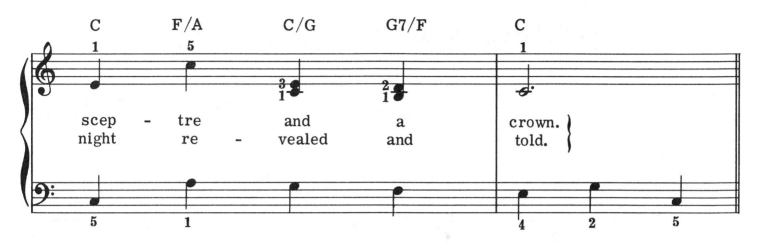

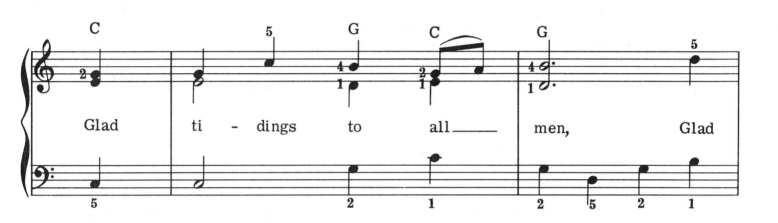

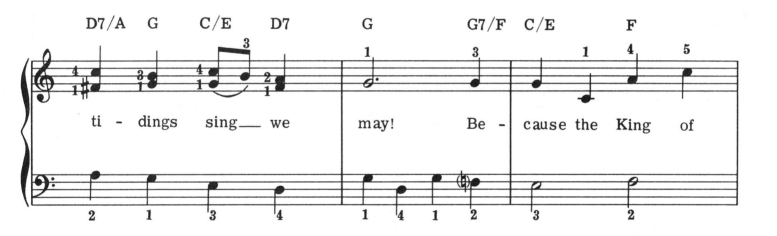

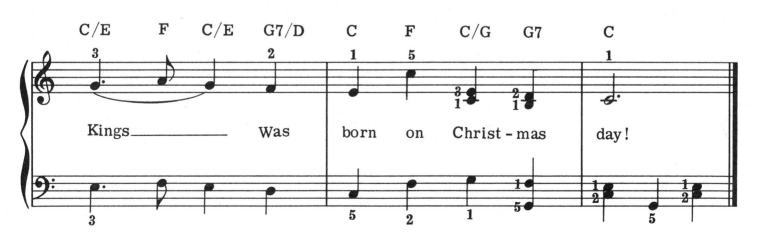

CHRISTMAS AULD LANG SYNE

Words and Music by
MANN CURTIS and FRANK MILITARY
Arranged by DAN COATES

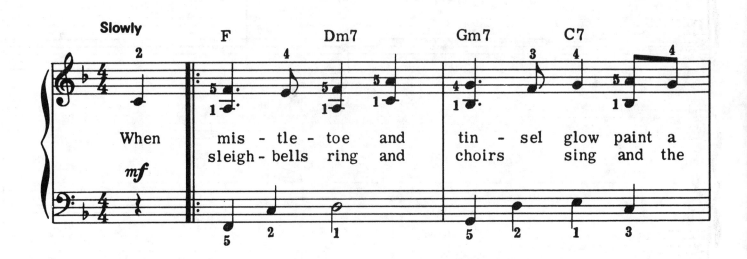

When mis - tle - toe and tin - sel glow paint a
sleigh - bells ring and choirs sing and the

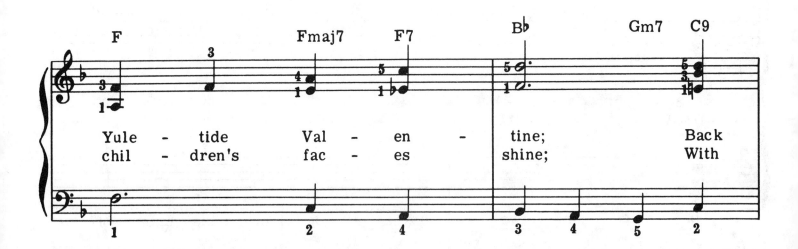

Yule - tide Val - en - tine; Back
chil - dren's fac - es shine; With

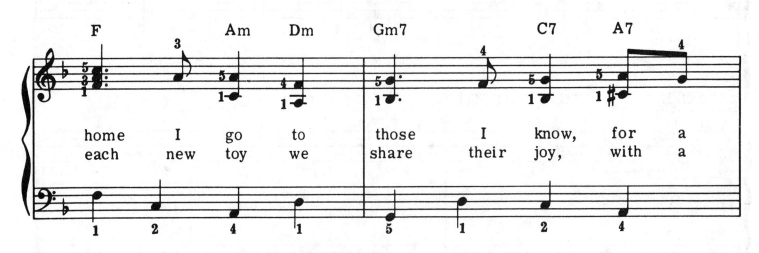

home I go to those I know, for a
each new toy we share their joy, with a

THE CHRISTMAS WALTZ

Words by
SAMMY CAHN

Music by
JULE STYNE
Arranged by DAN COATES

THE FIRST NOËL

Traditional English Carol
Arranged by DAN COATES

sheep   on a cold win - ter's   night____ that

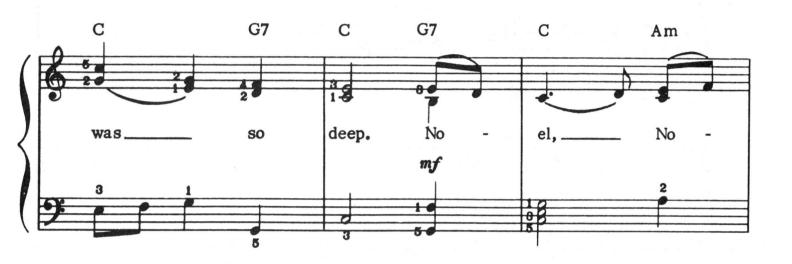

was____   so   deep.   No -   el,____   No -

mf

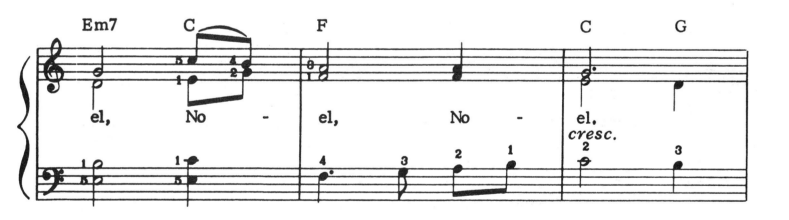

el,   No -   el,   No -   el.

cresc.

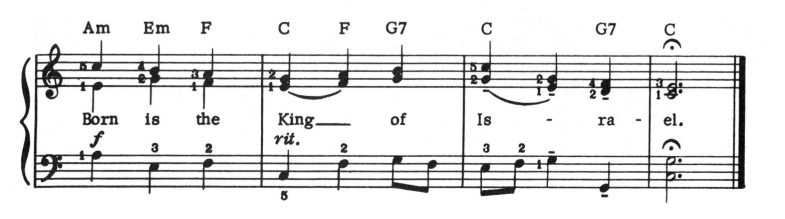

Born is the   King____ of   Is -   ra - el.

f   *rit.*

CHRISTMAS IN KILLARNEY

Words and Music by
JOHN REDMOND, JAMES CAVANAUGH
and FRANK WELDON
Arranged by DAN COATES

Moderately

The hol - ly green, the i - vy green, The

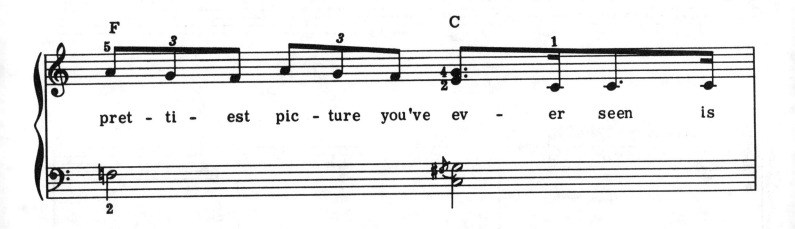

pret - ti - est pic - ture you've ev - er seen is

Christ-mas in Kil - lar - ney, With all of the folks at home. It's

nice you know, to kiss your beau while cud-dling un-der the mis-tle-toe, And

San-ta Claus, you know of course, is one of the boys from home. The

door is al-ways o-pen, The neigh-bors pay a call, and

Fa-ther John, be-fore he's gone, Will bless the house and all. How

GESU BAMBINO
(The Infant Jesus)

Words by
FREDERICK H. MARTENS

Music by
PIETRO A. YON
Arranged by DAN COATES

46

48

GATHER AROUND THE CHRISTMAS TREE

By
JOHN HOPKINS
Arranged by DAN COATES

Gath - er a - round the Christ - mas tree! Gath - er a - round the

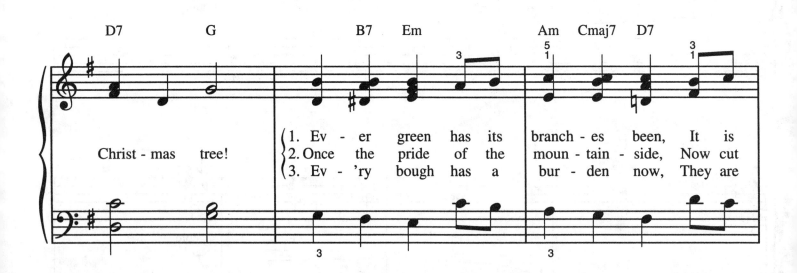

Christ - mas tree!

1. Ev - er green has its branch - es been, It is
2. Once the pride of the moun - tain - side, Now cut
3. Ev - 'ry bough has a bur - den now, They are

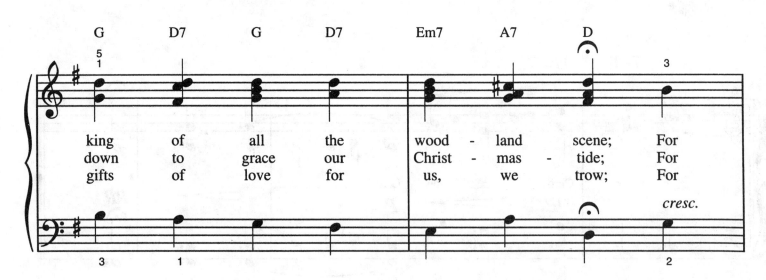

king of all the wood - land scene; For
down to grace our Christ - mas - tide; For
gifts of love for us, we trow; For

cresc.

GOD REST YE MERRY, GENTLEMEN

Traditional English Carol
Arranged by DAN COATES

Chorus

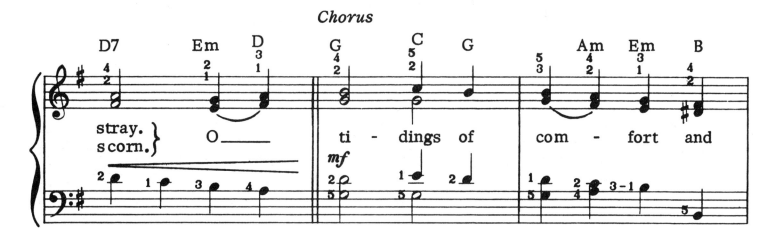

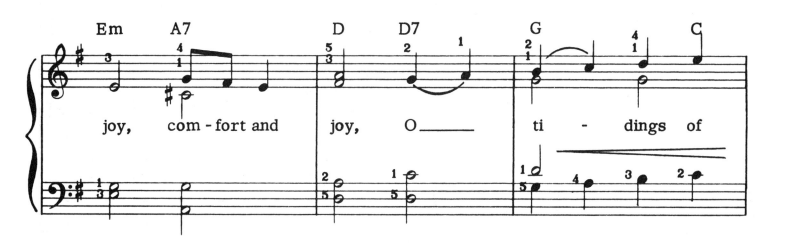

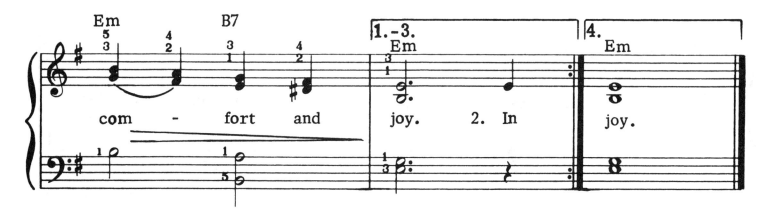

Additional Lyrics

3. From God our Heavenly Father, a blessed Angel came;
    And unto certain shepherds, brought tidings of the same;
    How that in Bethlehem was born the Son of God by name.

    (Chorus)

4. The shepherds at those tidings rejoiced much in mind,
    And left their flocks a-feeding, in tempest, storm, and wind,
    And went to Bethlehem straight-way, the Son of God to find.

    (Chorus)

GOOD KING WENCESLAS

Traditional English Carol
Arranged by DAN COATES

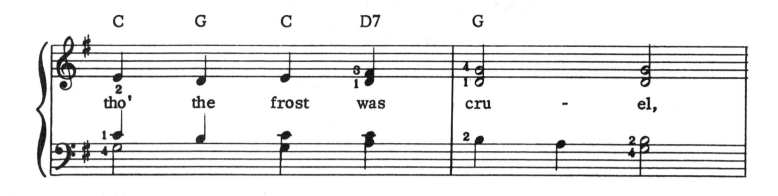

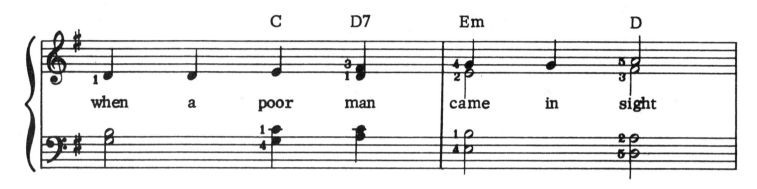

Additional Lyrics

2. "Hither, page, and stand by me, if thou know'st it, telling
   Yonder peasant, who is he? Where, and what his dwelling?"
   "Sire, he lives a good league hence, underneath the mountain;
   Right against the forest fence, by Saint Agnes Fountain."

3. "Bring me flesh and bring me wine, bring me pine logs hither;
   Thou and I will see him dine when we bear them thither."
   Page and monarch forth they went, forth they went together,
   Thro' the rude wind's wild lament and the bitter weather.

4. "Sire, the night is darker now, and the wind blows stronger.
   Fails my heart, I know not how, I can go no longer."
   "Mark my footsteps, my good page, tread, thou in them boldly:
   Thou shalt find the winter's rage freeze thy blood less coldly."

GRANDMA GOT RUN OVER
BY A REINDEER!

Words and Music by
RANDY BROOKS
Arranged by DAN COATES

Moderately bright

HARK! THE HERALD ANGELS SING

Words by
CHARLES WESLEY

Music by
FELIX MENDELSSOHN
Arranged by DAN COATES

Hark! the her - ald an - gels sing____

glo - ry to the new - born King.

Peace on earth, and mer - cy mild____

God and sin - ners re - con - ciled!

59

A HOLLY JOLLY CHRISTMAS

Words and Music by
JOHNNY MARKS
Arranged by DAN COATES

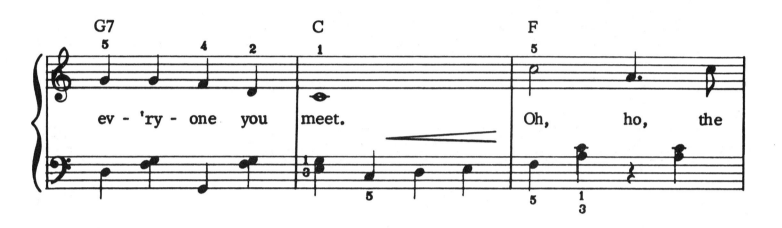

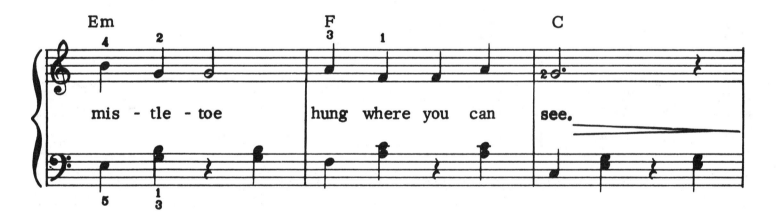

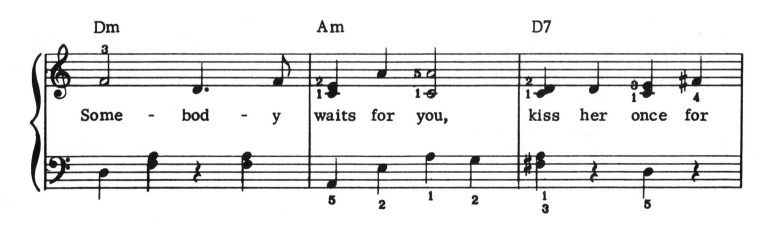

(There's No Place Like)
HOME FOR THE HOLIDAYS

Words by
AL STILLMAN

Music by
ROBERT ALLEN
Arranged by DAN COATES

64

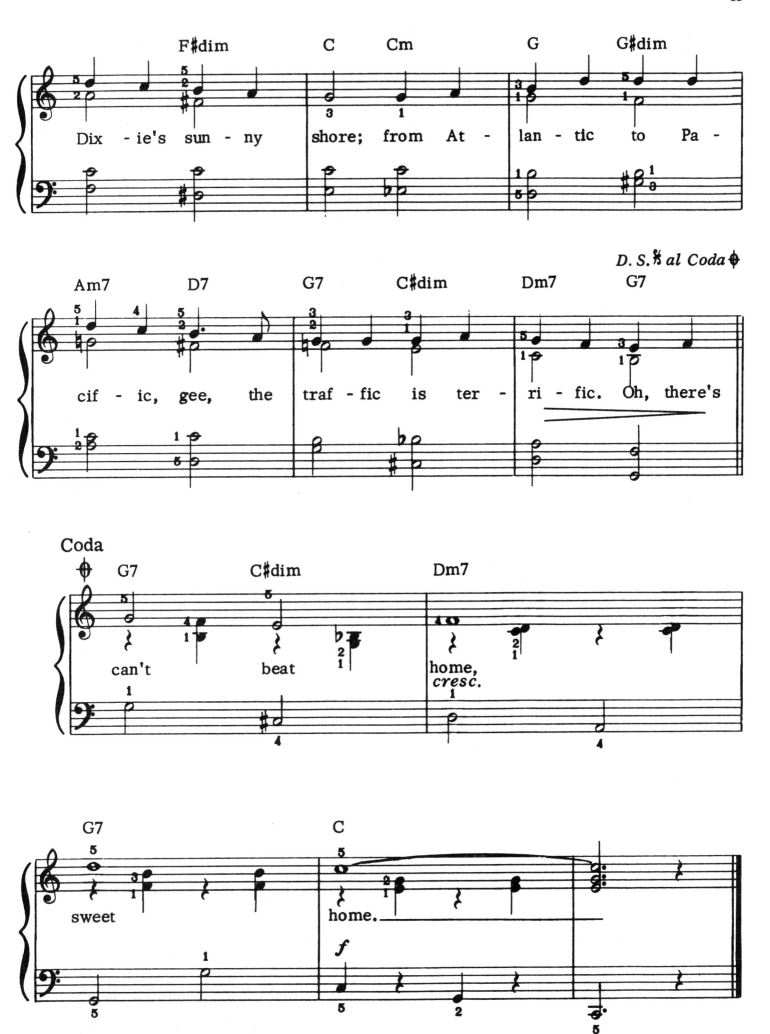

I HEARD THE BELLS ON CHRISTMAS DAY

Words by
HENRY WADSWORTH LONGFELLOW
(Adapted by JOHNNY MARKS)

Music by
JOHNNY MARKS
Arranged by DAN COATES

67

I SAW THREE SHIPS

Traditional English XV Century Legend
Arranged by DAN COATES

Additional Lyrics

3. The Virgin Mary and Christ were there,
   On Christmas Day, on Christmas Day;
   The Virgin Mary and Christ were there,
   On Christmas Day in the morning.

4. Then let us all rejoice amain,
   On Christmas Day, on Christmas Day;
   Then let us all rejoice amain,
   On Christmas Day in the morning.

INFANT SO GENTLE

Gascon Carol
Arranged by DAN COATES

IT CAME UPON THE MIDNIGHT CLEAR

Words by
EDMUND H. SEARS

Music by
RICHARD S. WILLIS
Arranged by DAN COATES

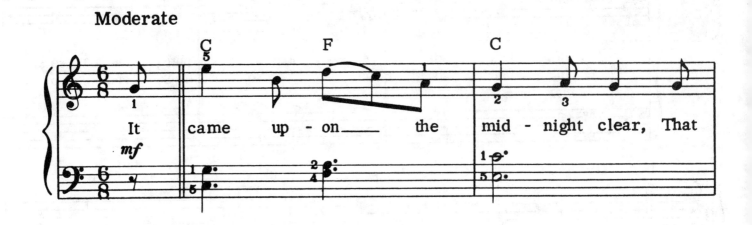

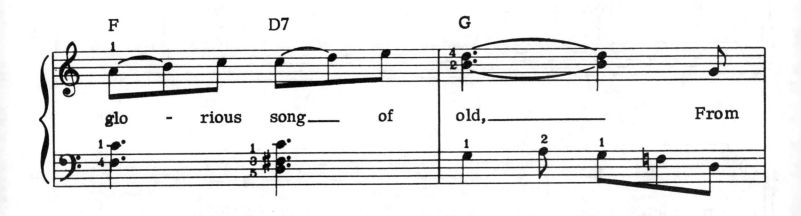

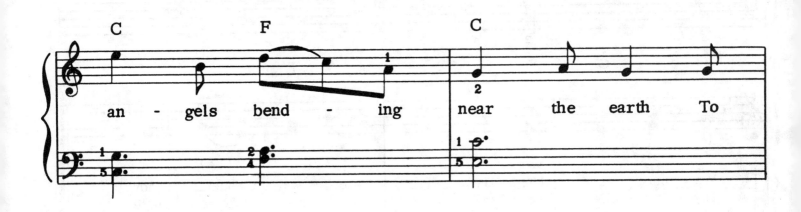

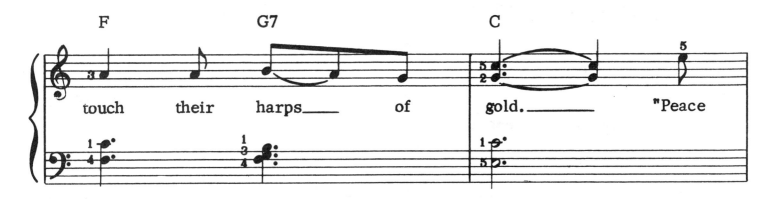

touch their harps___ of gold._____ "Peace

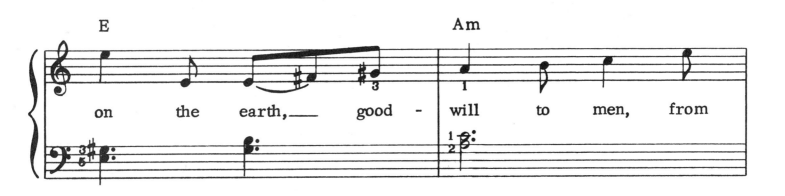

on the earth,___ good - will to men, from

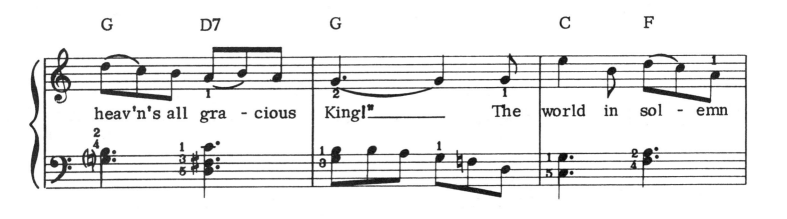

heav'n's all gra - cious King!"_____ The world in sol - emn

still - ness lay To hear the an - gels sing.

I'LL BE HOME FOR CHRISTMAS

Words by
KIM GANNON

Music by
WALTER KENT
Arranged by DAN COATES

THE LITTLE DRUMMER BOY

Words and Music by
KATHERINE DAVIS, HENRY ONORATI
and HARRY SIMEONE
Arranged by DAN COATES

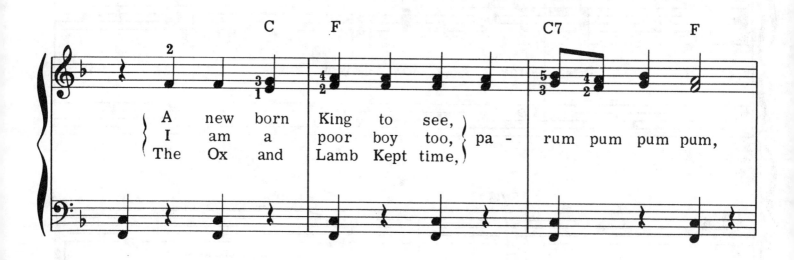

O HOLY NIGHT

Words and Music by
ADOLPHE ADAM
Arranged by DAN COATES

Moderately slow, even tempo

O Ho - ly Night!_____ The stars are bright - ly
shin - ing. It is the night of our dear Sav-ior's
birth. Long lay the world_____ in sin and er - ror
pin - ing till He ap - peared and the soul felt its

O CHRISTMAS TREE

(O Tannenbaum)

OLD GERMAN CAROL
Arranged by DAN COATES

Moderately

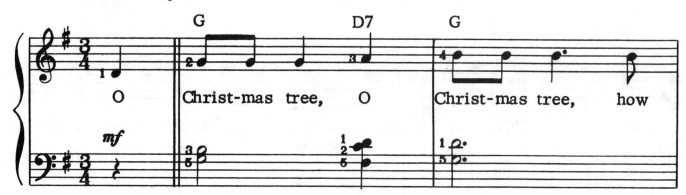

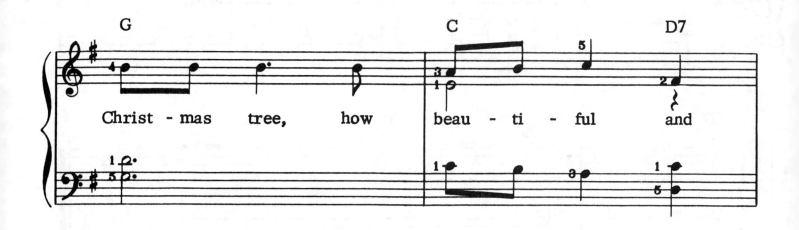

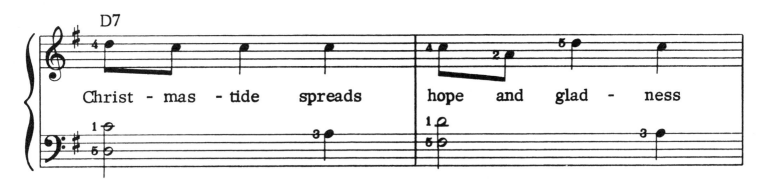

O COME, ALL YE FAITHFUL
(Adeste Fideles)

By
JOHN FRANCIS WADE
Arranged by DAN COATES

Moderate, steady tempo

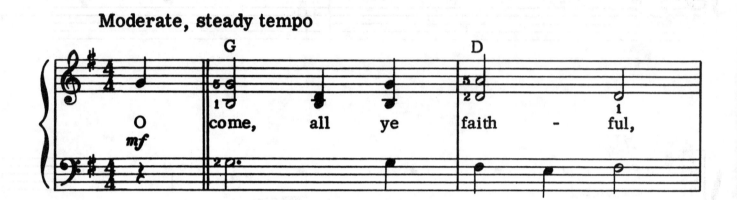

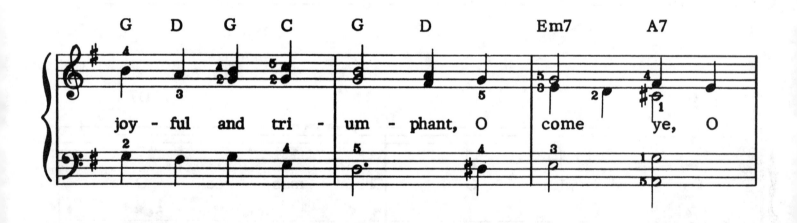

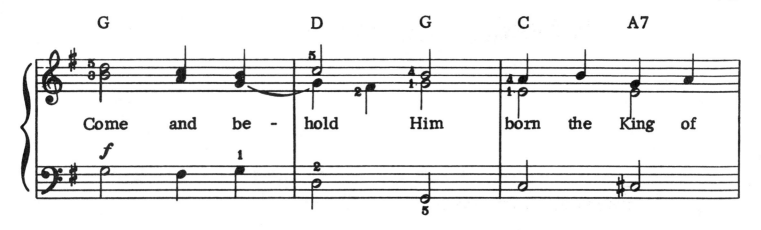

G   D   G   C   A7

Come   and   be - hold   Him   born   the   King   of

f

D   No chord

an - gels: O   come, let us a - dore Him, O

mp

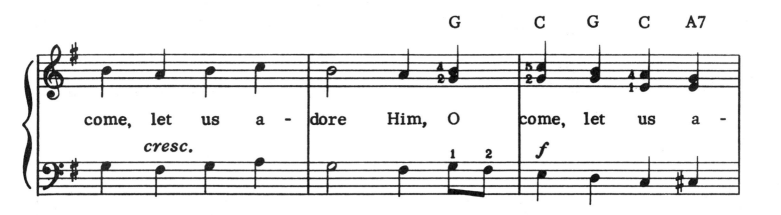

G   C G C A7

come, let us a - dore Him, O   come, let us a -

cresc.   *f*

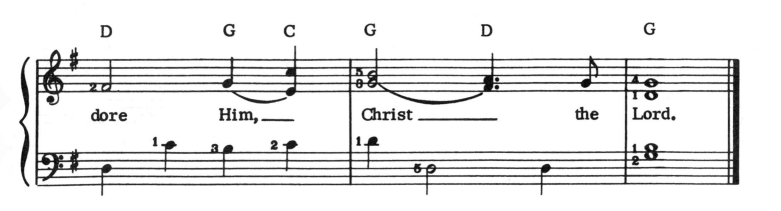

D   G C   G   D   G

dore   Him,   Christ   the Lord.

O COME, O COME EMMANUEL

Traditional
Arranged by DAN COATES

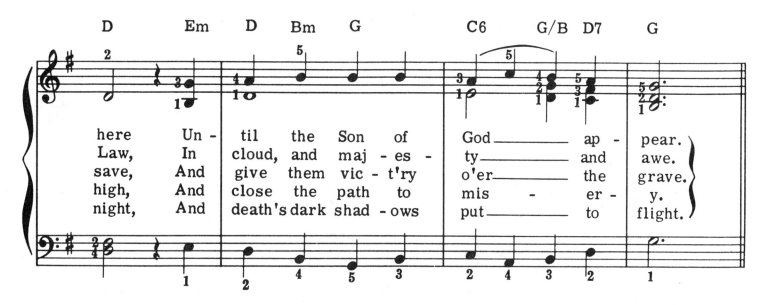

here   Un - til   the Son   of   God _____ ap - pear.
Law,   In   cloud, and maj - es - ty _____ and   awe.
save,   And give them vic - t'ry o'er _____ the grave.
high,   And close the path to   mis - er - y.
night,   And death's dark shad - ows put _____ to flight.

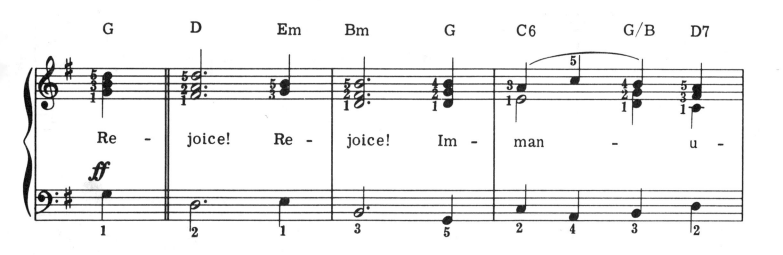

Re - joice! Re - joice! Im - man - u -

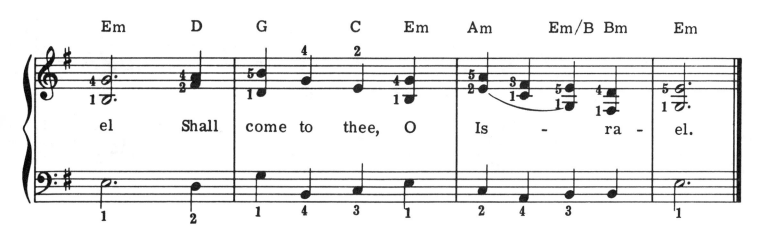

el   Shall come to thee, O   Is - ra - el.

O LITTLE TOWN OF BETHLEHEM

Words by
PHILLIPS BROOKS

Music by
LEWIS H. REDNER
Arranged by DAN COATES

(There's Nothing Like)
AN OLD FASHIONED CHRISTMAS

Words and Music by
JOHNNY MARKS
Arranged by DAN COATES

ROCKIN' AROUND
THE CHRISTMAS TREE

Words and Music by
JOHNNY MARKS
Arranged by DAN COATES

Moderately, with a rock

Rock-in' a - round the Christ-mas tree__ at the Christ-mas par - ty hop. Mis-tle-toe hung where you can see__ ev - 'ry cou - ple tries to stop. Rock-in' a - round the Christ-mas tree,__ let the Christ-mas spir - it

ring. Lat-er we'll have some pump-kin pie __ and we'll

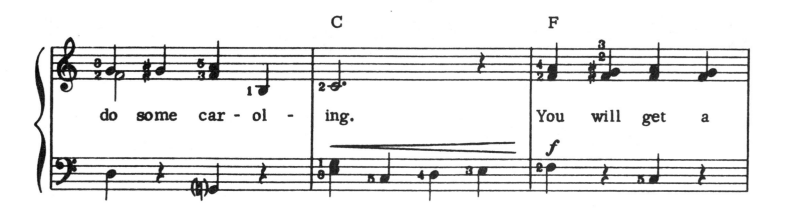

do some car - ol - ing. You will get a

sen - ti - men - tal feel - ing when you hear

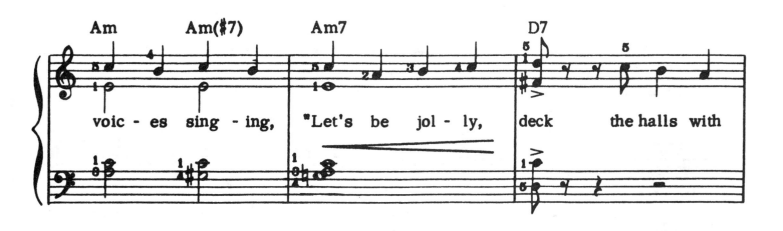

voic - es sing - ing, "Let's be jol - ly, deck the halls with

SILENT NIGHT

Words by
JOSEPH MOHR

Music by
FRANZ GRUBER
Arranged by DAN COATES

SING WE NOËL

French Carol
Arranged by DAN COATES

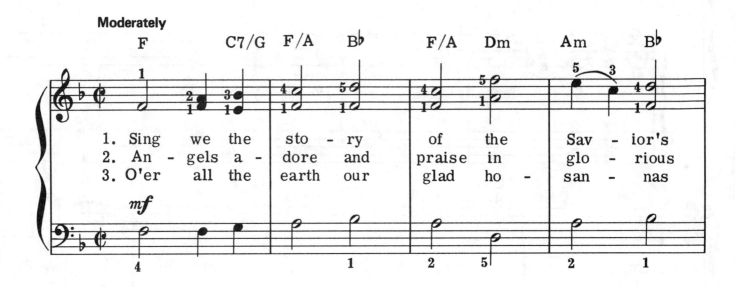

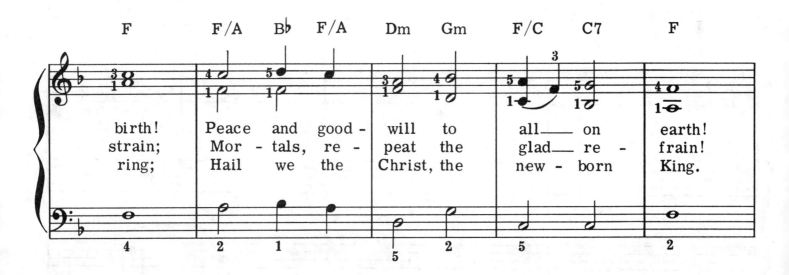

THERE IS NO CHRISTMAS
LIKE A HOME CHRISTMAS

Words by
CARL SIGMAN

Music by
MICKEY J. ADDY
Arranged by DAN COATES

TOYLAND

Words by
GLEN MAC DONOUGH

Music by
VICTOR HERBERT
Arranged by DAN COATES

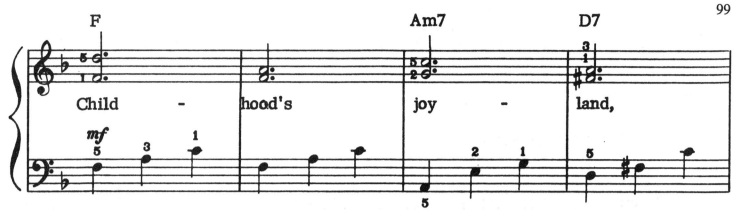

Child - hood's joy - land,

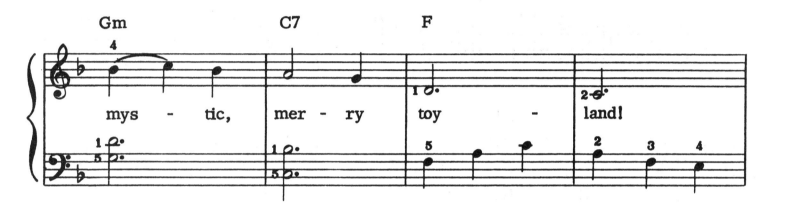

mys - tic, mer - ry toy - land!

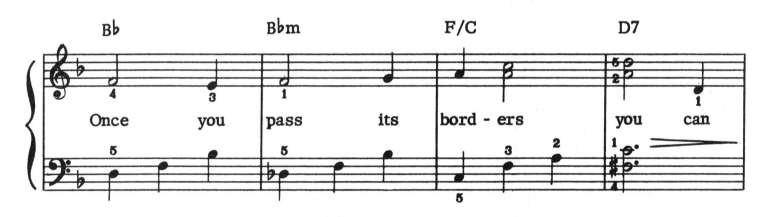

Once you pass its bord - ers you can

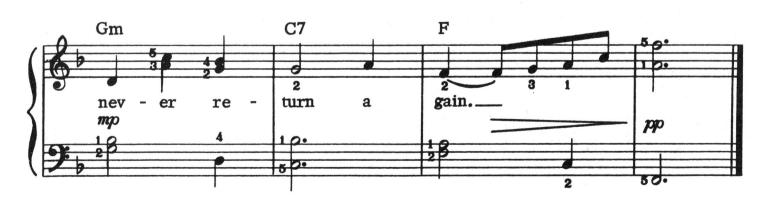

nev - er re - turn a - gain.

THE TWELVE DAYS OF CHRISTMAS

Old English
Arranged by DAN COATES

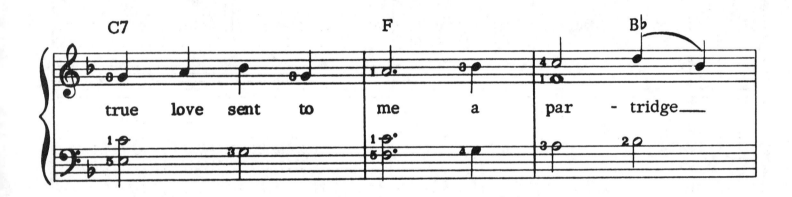

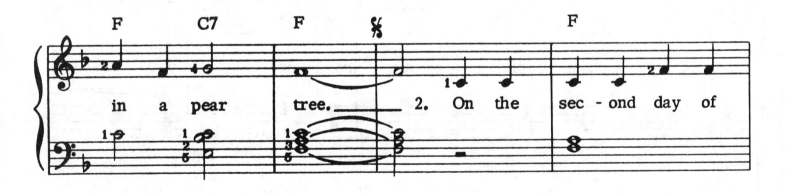

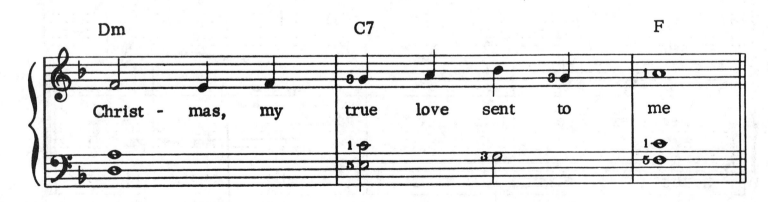

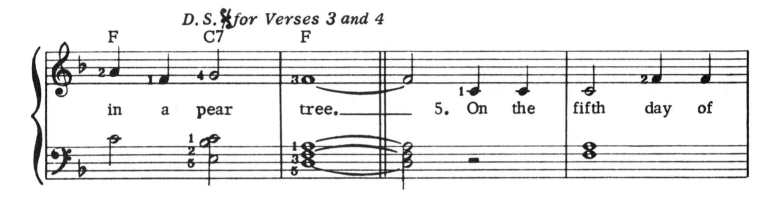

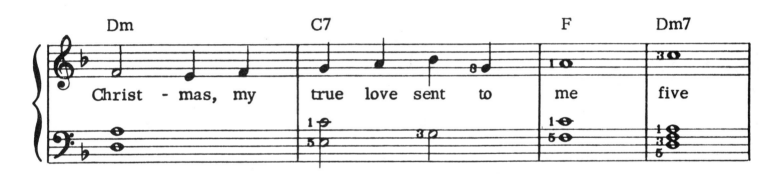

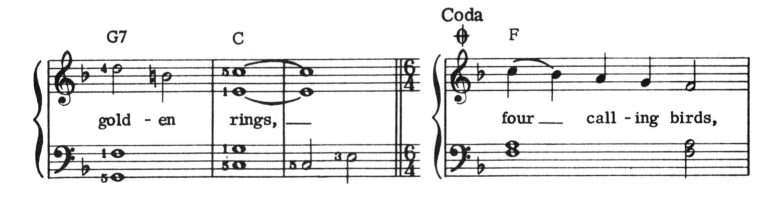

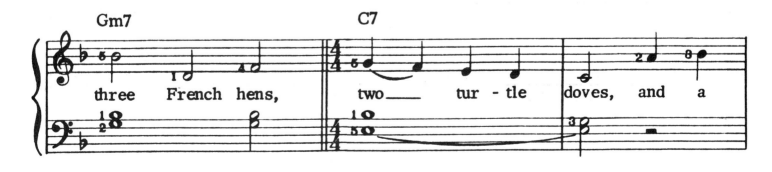

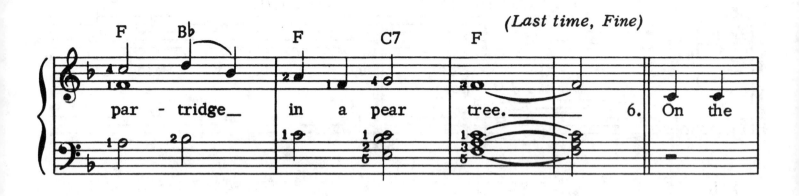

(Last time, Fine)

par - tridge   in a pear   tree.   6. On the

sixth day of   Christ- mas, my   true love sent to   me

To Coda
For Verses 6 to 12

six geese a -lay-ing,   five   gold - en   rings!

(Repeat as needed)

3. On the third ⎤
4. On the fourth ⎦ day of Christmas, my true love sent to me ⎡ two turtle doves
three French hens ⎤ and a part-
four calling birds ⎦ ridge in a
pear tree.

6. On the sixth ⎤
7. On the seventh
8. On the eighth
9. On the ninth ⎥ day of Christmas, my true love sent to me ⎡ six geese a-laying,
seven swans-a-swimming,
eight maids a-milking,
nine ladies dancing, ⎤ five
10. On the tenth
11. On the 'leventh
12. On the twelfth ⎦ ten lords a-leaping,
'leven pipers piping,
twelve drummers drumming, ⎦ golden rings

UP ON THE HOUSETOP

Words and Music by
BENJAMIN RUSSELL HANBY
Arranged by DAN COATES

WE THREE KINGS
OF ORIENT ARE

Traditional
Arranged by DAN COATES

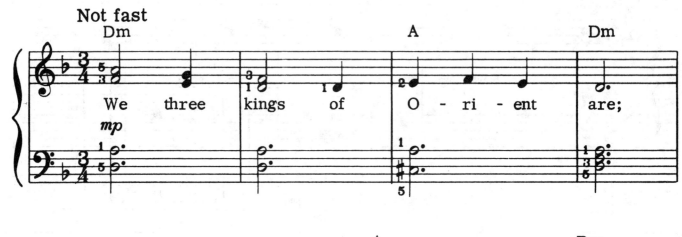

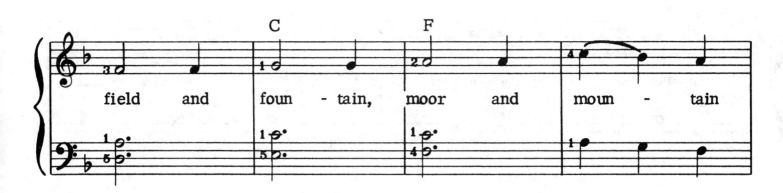

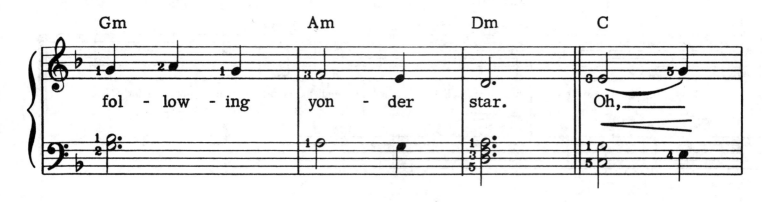

Star of won - der, star of night, star with roy - al beau - ty bright, west - ward lead - ing, still pro - ceed - ing, guide us to Thy per - fect light.

Additional Lyrics

2. Born a King on Bethlehem's plain,
   Gold I bring, to crown Him again,
   King forever, ceasing never
   Over us all to reign:

3. Frankincense to offer have I,
   Incense owns a Deity nigh.
   Prayer and praising, all men raising
   Worship Him, God most high:

4. Myrrh is mine, its bitter perfume
   Breathes a life of gathering gloom;
   Sorrowing, sighing, bleeding, dying,
   Sealed in the stone-cold tomb:

5. Glorious now behold Him arise,
   King and God and sacrifice!
   Heaven sings Alleluia,
   Alleluia the earth replies:

WHAT CHILD IS THIS?

Traditional
Arranged by DAN COATES

Additional Lyrics

2. Why lies He in such mean estate,
   Where ox and ass are feeding?
   Good Christian fear, for sinners here
   The silent word is pleading.
   Nails, spear shall pierce Him thru;
   The Cross be born for me, for you,
   Hail, hail the word made flesh,
   The Babe, the Son of Mary.

3. So bring Him incense, gold and myrrh,
   Come peasant, king to own Him.
   The King of Kings salvation brings;
   Let loving hearts enthrone Him.
   Raise, raise the song on high
   The Virgin sings her lullaby;
   Joy, joy for Christ is born,
   The Son of Mary.

WE WISH YOU A MERRY CHRISTMAS

Traditional English Folk Song
Arranged by DAN COATES

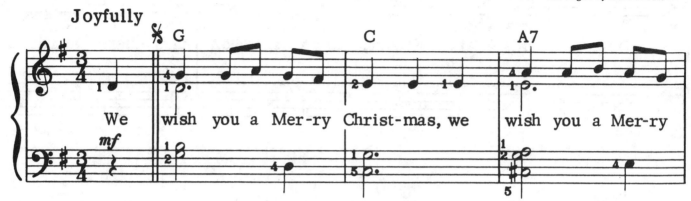

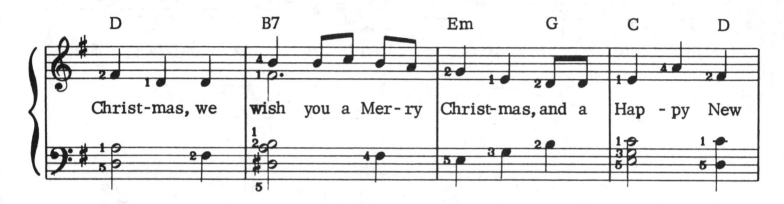

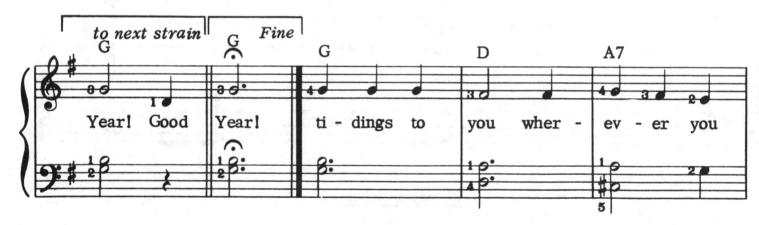

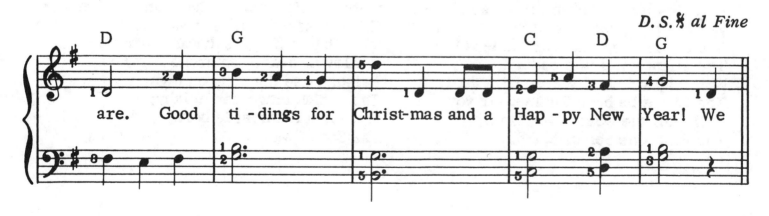